Encountering
Bare-Bones
Christianity

Encountering Bare-Bones Christianity

Jost Zetzsche

Encountering Bare-Bones Christianity

ISBN: 978-1-0879-8765-1

Printed in the United States of America

*Dedicated to Anna, Hannes,
and Lara*

*Also dedicated to
Ashton, Bailey, Berit, Emily, Gabby,
Grace, Graham, Hannah S.,
Hannah R., Jasper, Jochen, Josh,
Kuahman, Lily, Lotte, Mo, Tara,
and Wiebke*

This little book has a simple purpose: to explain in easily understandable terms what my life as a Christian has meant for me and how it is different from the life I led before. My hope is that it will provide you with positive practical evidence of the difference it makes to live a life that follows Jesus.

But let me first introduce myself. I am a middle-aged man who lives in a foreign country. I am married to a woman who is much more equipped with talents than I, our three children are adults and all in the process of independently carving out their lives, and I have two dogs. I take comfort that I'm definitely smarter than my dogs (though people seem inclined to praise their cuteness much more than they praise mine).

I have an impressive-sounding academic degree, but I have always felt a bit of a scholarly impostor. I earned my degree through hard work but not necessarily great brilliance. I do think I have two mental strengths, though, if you want to call them that: I tend to be persistent if something feels relevant to me, and I tend to have good ideas. I hope this book is one of those good ideas, followed persistently.

I embraced the Christian faith as an adult. I remember the room I was in, the chair I was sitting in, and the mixture of dread and anticipation that filled me before I made that step. It felt like a jump off a high-dive platform. Unlike a painful belly flop, though, the results instead threatened to irreversibly change the direction of my life.

I did end up jumping, and my life has indeed taken a different course. But I've realized over time that this radical step of conversion is only one avenue for embracing the Christian faith. There are as many different ways to choose the Christian faith as there are Christians. For many, in fact, a careful step-by-step approach that weighs the risks and benefits to becoming a Christian is much more natural and reasonable than the radical now-or-never approach.

I've also realized that though I've never been bashful to share that I *have* faith since taking that plunge, I never actually *explained* my faith by communicating what specific differences it makes in my life. For someone who is more likely to take a step-by-step approach, an explanation like that might be helpful. This book is my attempt to do just that.

It's important to note at this point that I'm not a theologian. I am a Christian believer who is curious about and confident in what I believe, and that's what I'm going to talk about: my intimate experience with faith and the benefits—the actual advantages—that this Christian faith holds for me and for many other Christians.

When I say "Christian" I'm not referring to a kind of faith that is primarily rooted in culture or tradition, a faith that consists of purely ritualistic acts. Instead, I'm talking about faith that is focused on the life-changing reality of Jesus. I'll explain more of what that means later. I'm also not particularly interested in labels like Protestant, Orthodox, or Catholic, and certainly not in the many sub-groups that fall under those broad categories.

Depending on where you live and how you grew up, being a Christian might reflect the norm around you, or it might be something completely counter-cultural. Either way, it may not be surrounded with many positive connotations. If you're in the first group, I hope to communicate that while there might be a lot of people around you who define themselves as Christian, and some of them just seem like regular and boring people, Christianity is neither commonplace nor boring. It's radical, exciting, and, yes, *really* counter-cultural. If you're in the second group, I hope to unveil the same radical, exciting, and maybe unexpected nature of the Christian faith.

I clearly don't know what you specifically think about Christianity, but according to my experience, people who are skeptical about or indifferent toward the Christian faith often share some or all of these opinions:

- I equate it with "doing good," but I see too many examples of Christians who don't act that way.

- I look at the long history of the Christian church (including the church today) and how it has allowed itself to be politicized and complicit in committing terrible wrongs.

- I don't really want to spend time with the kind of "conventional" people who go to church (not to mention the hypocritical kind!).

I'm talking about faith that is focused on the life-changing reality of Jesus. I'm also not particularly interested in labels like Protestant, Orthodox, or Catholic, and certainly not in the many sub-groups that fall under those broad categories.

- I shake my head in disbelief that people in the 21st century still believe in something that seems to defy science and reason.

- I can't accept that the Bible, a book written at least 2,000 years ago and for a completely different people, can have a real impact on someone who lives in the 21st century.

- I might believe in a "higher power," but I don't want it (or myself) to be put into a specifically defined box.

- I'm just too busy to commit to something that doesn't seem truly relevant.

- I was badly hurt by people from the church.

Aside from the last one—and I'm very, very sorry if that applies to you—I can personally relate to all of these points. I get them. So I encourage you to keep reading to see how these entirely valid reasons can be untangled, like the string in a large knot, by the radical nature of

Christianity. (Notice I didn't say "the radical nature of Christians!")

Of course, this is somewhat different for those who have been hurt. Hurts don't untangle easily, and if they do, the untangling doesn't happen only in the head. Perhaps by the end of the book we may be able to agree that it was *people* who did the hurting rather than "the church."

How can we even talk about faith?

Faith is a nebulous and strange thing, especially for those who have never consciously experienced anything like it. In some ways, faith is the very opposite of fact-based knowledge. In a sense—a sense that is maddening to those who don't have faith—it is both weaker and stronger than facts.

It's weaker because it eludes the scientific process. Take gravity, for instance. Gravity is something that is real and scientifically proven. While we might not grasp all the scientific facts that make it work, we see it in action every single minute of our lives. We can

In some ways, faith is the very opposite of fact-based knowledge. In a sense—a sense that is maddening to those who don't have faith—it is both weaker and stronger than facts.

trust gravity, and it can always be replicated. It is so much a part of our reality that we rarely even think about it. Gravity is one of the laws that define our environment and therefore us, all of us and all the time.

Clearly, the realities of faith are different. They are completely hidden from those who don't share the faith. They are so hidden, in fact, that those who claim to have faith elicit a variety of reactions from those who don't, everything from ridicule and pity to envy and admiration. For those with faith, however, the realities of faith are not only real but represent an ultimate reality, a reality beyond reality.

It's frustrating that the gap between faith and no faith cannot be proven by science (or more fundamentally: by smell, sound, taste, touch, or sight). Even more, our language—the very vehicle through which we want to communicate it—fails us.

There are two reasons behind this failure. First, words need to have a common point of reference between the speaker and the listener. If that commonality is missing, words create misunderstandings. But there is also another perhaps even more acute reason why communication often fails. I can choose to use words to describe my faith that are commonly used in the non-faith realm (words like "trust," "hope," "love," "community," "joy," and, yes, even "faith"). Because of their wide usage, however, these words may imply a different reality than I intended. Or I can use religious words that are highly specialized and therefore meaningless because my listener simply has no point of reference to understand them (words like "baptism" or "sanctification").

If words could communicate seamlessly, the Christian scriptures might read something like this:

I am God and I created you. I want you to be with me, but since you—and everyone else—are not yet as complete as you'd have to be to be in my presence, I need you to accept that I in the form of Jesus have taken it upon myself to die for your shortcomings. Accept that, love according to the guidance of the spirit that I'll give you once you accept it, and you'll be with me forever.

That's it.

Does that mean anything to anyone except those who are deeply familiar with the Christian faith? Of course not. Not only do the words ring hollow ("created me," "complete," "shortcomings," "spirit," and, yes, "God"), but the whole message seems bizarre at best, unhinged at worst.

To avoid these misunderstandings, I'd like to try talking about faith not in an abstract sense but as something with a real and mea-surable impact on areas of life that all people share. With that as our point of reference, communication might actually be possible.

  We all have emotions surrounding ideas about

- loneliness (I talk about this on page 21),

- community (page 29),

- life's purpose (page 43),

- our true selves (page 53),

- our place in the world (page 69),

- beauty and the planet (page 77),

- understanding our life stories in a larger context (page 91),

- thankfulness (page 109),

- life's value (page 115),

- forgiveness (page 129),

- suffering (page 137),

- aging (page 149),

- and death (page 161).

I have experienced a profound difference in how I perceive each of these realities since I embraced the Christian faith, and that is what motivates me to find language that expresses that difference for you.

So, if you're reluctant to go on that practical faith journey with me, you can stop right here and give this book to someone else. Either way, I'm so glad to have met you!

Here are some disclaimers

I can't speak for anyone else, and I'm certainly not a spokesperson for "Christianity" or any other "Christian" aside from myself. I feel that in general I have a good idea of how I should conduct my life (which doesn't necessarily mean I always do conduct it in that way), what role God plays in my life, and what the Bible talks about. To some degree we are all products of our environment, and what I have to say is naturally also shaped by the people I have been with, the books I've read, and my own spiritual practices. Still I hope that what you'll find in these pages represents a view that is common among many Christians of the various confessions and denominations.

The other disclaimer is probably even more important. I will often say "Christians believe ..." and "Christians don't believe ...." I have a feeling I know exactly what will happen if someone reads this who is not very familiar with the Christian faith but has rubbed shoulders with Christians or people who claim to be Christian. That person will likely be completely confused or—more likely—angry about the large gulf between what Christianity claims for its followers and what the followers end up doing with it.

I know!

If you're one of those: Yes, you're completely right. It's true: Most Christians (myself included) are not doing particularly well when it comes to living and sharing and demonstrating exactly what it means to be a Christian. Most of us are pretty much just like anyone else when it comes to being particularly good or bad about achieving what we set out to do. When I say "pretty much," I mean that there actually is one difference. We believe that God helps us process our failures (we'll talk about that when we discuss forgiveness later on). And while our failures might still hurt our pride, this belief allows us to keep trying, giving us the hope that eventually we might *actually* get better at whatever we're trying to do.

Maybe it will help your frustration with Christians to imagine the church being as much a center for worship and community as it is a hospital for the sick and wounded. Not only for those who are more wounded than those outside the church, but for anyone anywhere along the entire human spectrum of woundedness.

I find that image liberating. Perhaps you will, too.

Most Christians (myself included) are not doing particularly well when it comes to living and sharing and demonstrating exactly what it means to be a Christian.

I find an answer
to my deep
and undefined
loneliness

Faith is deeply personal. It touches areas of your inner being that, if you don't know faith, simply remain untouched. People in the church have come up with a lot of descriptions for this (like the "Jesus-shaped hole in all of us"), but the best way I can explain it is with the concept of the soulmate, the "other, actual half" that Plato refers to.

My wife Kristen and I are happily married. Both of us feel that we are good matches for each other, increasingly so the longer we're together. But do we believe that we are each other's "soulmate" in the sense that there could have been no one else for us? I don't think so. Both she and I could also have tried this investment with someone else—and it

23

might have worked. Or not. It's not exactly a romantic image, but maybe a hopeful one because no one has to worry that they've missed the only one they were destined to spend their life with.

Still, it continues to amaze me how increasingly closely Kristen and I are aligned. I see something while driving in the car and I don't even have to point it out to her before starting to talk about it. I know that she has also noticed it. I know when she feels happy, when she's nervous or excited, often even when I'm not with her.

I don't think I'm describing anything extraordinary here. It's what happens when you spend 30 years living with each other and caring for one another.

But do I know everything about her? Do I understand every little change in mood or every thought that goes through her head? Clearly not. And I know the same is true for her as she sees and knows me.

In my late teens and early 20s, there was no topic that occupied my thoughts and emotions more than the concept of loneliness. I was neither super popular nor super unpopular. I had good friends, and still I felt completely lonely. I felt—I knew—that I was not able to fully share who I really was with anyone. In fact, I had this ongoing vision of *literally* opening up my chest so I could show people what was in my heart and what I was truly made of. Since that was not possible, I filled journal after journal with my thoughts on my isolation. That relieved the pain of loneliness a little, but it could not resolve it. It was a loneliness that went far beyond words and images. It was a sense of complete isolation—even from myself. I sensed all those feelings and longings inside of me, but since I could not even share them with myself, let alone someone else, were they really real?

I'm sure that not everyone experiences loneliness in the same way I did, but I do think everyone experiences some of it. It only makes sense. We are complex beings, more complex than we ourselves can completely comprehend or express. At the same time, we're also deeply social beings who are constantly looking for counterparts to share and be with.

Christians are convinced that we have an answer to this: We believe God knows us at an unspeakably deep level.

This is "unspeakable" in the truest sense of the word, this central place that cannot be expressed with words, with paintings, sculptures, or songs, but still cries out to be seen and heard. Why? Well, there are two options. Either we exist with an eternal place of longing and despair, one that does not have a possible counterpart. Or, and this is what Christians believe, there actually is a reason for that deep and hidden place in all of us: it's the place that is there to be known and understood by God.

This has been my personal experience. I suspect that no one who has ever made that jump into becoming a Christian, into a relationship with God, knew what the results of that decision would be. For me, the greatest surprise was an almost immediate sense of relief. The burden that I had carried with me

We believe God knows us at an unspeakably deep level. This is "unspeakable" in the truest sense of the word, this central place that cannot be expressed with words, with paintings, sculptures, or songs, but still cries out to be seen and heard.

all my thinking life, the pressure that had continued to build and wanted to be released into a relationship that would adequately respond to that longing, happened to be God.

Why? Any answer to that might seem somewhat trivial or cliché. All I know is that I had come home. Without being familiar with any theological or biblical reasoning, I knew it was real. I had understood that the only one who could understand my wordless expression and call for community was God. It felt so clear that it was designed that way.

Since then I have learned that the Bible spends a lot of time discussing the intimate ways that God knows each one of us and understands us—words or no words. I expect that in 10 or 20 years, Kristen's and my intimacy and knowledge of each other will have become even more profound. But it will be a lesser familiarity and trust than either of us continues to experience as we turn toward God.

I discover true community with others

While the kind of community that Christians experience with God is unique and unrivaled by any relationship, there is another kind of relationship that is unique as well, though it's different and not quite as seamless and intimate. I'm talking about relationships to other Christians within the church (here I mean "church" as a local group of Christians meeting regularly).

Let me first talk about some of the reasons why it's not always seamless before addressing why this community ends up being one of the most treasured benefits in my life.

As I said before, Christians are anything but perfect. First, Christianity embraces the truth that people—we—are essentially incapable of dealing with our shortcomings on our own. These shortcomings—like selfishness, greed, and pride—keep following us throughout our lives as Christians. Still, with God's help the goal is to learn to overcome them. In "learning to overcome," the emphasis is really more on the "learning" than on the "overcoming," at least as a realistically achievable goal. If I look at my own experience as a Christian who is eagerly trying to shed those shortcomings while also completely and exclusively embracing a new kind of identity, I can look back and celebrate some achievements. But as far as completely and always succeeding with that new and always-loving identity? Give me another 600 years and we'll talk again. No, seriously, Christians don't believe in achievable perfection in this life, and that has a tremendous impact on how we are with other Christians. We know nobody's perfect.

This means that some of the divisiveness of "normal" life can be part of church life as well. In the US, one of the greatest dividers occurs along ethnic lines, manifesting itself in quasi-segregated churches. This is partly a painful reminder of the history—and current presence—of racism in this country, but it is also a recognition that different church cultures have emerged between ethnic groups that are hard to bridge.

With that in mind, local churches still tend to be extremely diverse, and much more so than other groups based on interest. I'm particularly talking diversity in age, social standing, or political opinion.

And since I mentioned "political opinion," allow me one other comment about an area that Christians cannot be proud of: Throughout history, individual churches and sometimes the church as a whole have shown embarrassingly poor judgment regarding their partisan political entanglement. The involvement by some churches here in the US during the last several years is no exception to that. Still, it does not mean that local churches have to be divided. I'm a perfect example of that: I was brought up in Northern Europe with its rather progressive ideas about politics and society. These stand in sharp contrast to the opinion of many in rural America, and yet I am welcomed and loved in my local church here in rural Oregon.

Diversity is certainly possible for communities that are organized around interests as well, but according to my experience that's typically just not the case. As I watch people in so many societies around the world becoming increasingly fragmented—politically, culturally, and socioeconomically—I don't think there's much hope for an increase of diversity in interest-based groups. Those interests by definition serve to divide us.

In contrast, faith is not an interest that you pursue because of your social position, your ethnic background, your generational belonging, or your ideas on how politics and society should work. Faith goes deeper.

The Bible uses an image for the church that is very instructive: The church is compared to a living body, with Jesus as its head. That's important for a number of reasons. One is that this is an image or illustration of diversity. Just as various body parts have different and equally important roles to play, so do the different people within the church.

Especially at this point in time, our cultures typically consider diversity to be a positive and desirable attribute. One of the hallmarks of the Christian faith is equality between genders, poor and rich, people from different origins and different levels of education. (Just in case this rubs you wrong, I'll talk more about it down below.) Still, this does not come without a cost. As beautiful as diversity is, it's not always easy to be with everyone, especially those who are diametrically opposed to us in their cultural, societal, or generational

Faith is not an interest that you pursue because of your social position, your ethnic background, your generational belonging, or your ideas on how politics and society should work. Faith goes deeper.

outlook. The reason why Christians overall (and there clearly are exceptions) manage to be successful with the diversity in their local church is that we can disagree on all kinds of things, but not the love that we are supposed to show our neighbor—really, anyone we encounter—and particularly our fellow believers.

To me, this is one of the most challenging and most "complete" benefits of being a Christian, especially now that most of us don't live in communities of large and extended, multi-generational families or in other kinds of close-knit communities. The analogy with the family is not as random as it might sound. Old-fashioned Christians actually still call other Christians "sisters" or "brothers." While this might feel cheesy, it reflects a spiritual reality we believe in. Think about it: It's a great way to describe a fellow body part (and much less awkward than calling you a toe, a buttock, or a spleen). Instead, we're fellow family members in the family of God's children.

Christians believe that every person was

created by God and therefore belongs to God's community in an equal manner. But we also believe that every one of those loved creations needs to embrace God out of their own free will to become a family member, a part of that diverse, always slightly struggling (remember: people!), but intensely close-knit community.

I can't tell you how much I've learned from people who are significantly much older and people who are significantly much younger than I in that community. I've grown so much from people who are not nearly as econom- ically privileged as I am or who are much wealthier (and it has changed me to see the latter helping the former). I've been educated by others with virtually no education and their profound and simple (but not simplistic!) way of embracing the Christian faith as well as by brilliant Christian thinkers who were able to point out and explain intricacies of our faith that I could never have come up with on my own. I've been supported graciously and compassionately when my family needed it, and I've learned how joyful it can be to do the same for others when they are in a situation of need. I've been enriched to learn from others whose hobbies and interests are diametrically opposed to mine, people I would never really have otherwise noticed.

And here is the wild part, one that goes beyond the local community: Though sometimes confusing, it has been breathtaking to experience other communities of Christians expressing their "family life with God" in the way they show God and each other their love and their reverence. Even more unexplainable, I feel like I come home when I enter any kind of church. It's home because it's mine: it belongs to me and I to it. It might be a church of a completely different branch of Christianity, one that I have never seen before, in a country that I'm visiting for the first time, and yet it's mine and the community that meets there can claim me just as much. It's like the sense of ownership you might have regarding your country or your hometown. The beauty of its landscapes fill you with particular pride because it's "yours."

A last point about the local community of believers and its family aspect: We would not be who we are if not for our biological families, in a good sense as well as sometimes in a destructive sense. But no matter how good and supportive your biological family is, there is none that has not had or will not have struggles. Naturally that's true for church families as well.

People have the natural tendency to look out for themselves first. Yes, we hope our faith as Christians will counter and eventually change that. But if we imagine the local church as a place for injured people, injured by their selfishness and lack of love, who come to be made better, then we should expect a lot of people in different stages of healing (I referred to that earlier as the emphasis on "learning" rather than actually "overcoming"). With that in mind, we can also understand that there are going to be difficult relationships, especially given all the diversity and the great range of people we find. But because there is that sense of a family, very often those difficulties can either be overcome or we can accept that we don't have to be best friends with everyone—just like in our real family.

But just like in our biological family, we might have bonds with our siblings or cousins that don't seem to completely make sense—we're so different when it comes to interests or age, yet there is still a strong bond of love and trust. You will find relationships in the church that are similar to that. While this may not happen overnight, there is a great likelihood it will. We could call this supernatural, but I think it actually isn't. Maybe, in fact, it's completely natural.

After all, many in the church share a relationship with someone—God—that goes deeper than any other relationship they've ever had. It doesn't seem surprising that having that shared commonality opens up a lot of possibilities for deep conversations and a kind of communion that is far beyond the ordinary.

In fact, I have found this to be a level of intimacy that I just had not experienced before, creating relationships that are both deeper

But just like in our biological family, we might have bonds with our siblings or cousins that don't seem to completely make sense— we're so different when it comes to interests or age, yet there is still a strong bond of love and trust. You will find relationships in the church that are similar to that.

and wider. It is remarkable especially with someone who is really different from me, who can help me and whom I can help to grow as a person.

This is what I have found Christian friendships to be like. It's not that they're perfect and never change. It's not that they never disappoint. They have a tendency to be intense. And I no longer want to be without them in my life.

I understand life's ultimate purpose

The purpose of life is probably one of the two or three most-often asked questions in the stillness of the bedroom, in the despair of adolescence before entering the machinery of adult life, in times of pain—separation, death, depression, loneliness—but also in times of exuberance and overflowing joy. How do you answer that overwhelming question?

One way to respond is by pointing to causes, especially those that are rooted in objective needs: poverty, the environment, education, racial justice. The list could be continued on and on. To engage ourselves in these areas does indeed give meaning, especially if it's a sustained and ongoing effort.

Christians agree, and we do engage in trying to alleviate some of that pain. But we would not call this the meaning of life.

Another response to the question of life's purpose would be to point to relationships. Look at your parents, your spouse, your children, your friends, your colleagues, your classmates. These are the people who are around you, whom you love (or should love), relationships that you know could be so much better if you continue to work on them. If you have a spouse (or partner), the relationship with them is something that you will spend the rest of your life working on. That huge task will require endless amounts of energy and countless hours of negotiation (and, yes, will hopefully also result in more and more blissful moments, hours, and days).

Both children and parents can be a blessing, but in virtually all cases they also provide stumbling blocks. Events or behavioral patterns from the past have to be addressed and often forgiven, and it's difficult to navigate the relationship as children mature and parents age. This takes a lot of energy and time. So much so that it sometimes seems to fill a life— and give it purpose. Add to that the ongoing effort of building, maintaining, and repairing relationships to others around you, and you can easily understand that that's certainly one of the ways for anyone to define the meaning of life: to love and be loved.

Christians agree with that, with the one difference that we would say this is not the meaning of life but one of its outcomes.

A third way might be to point to yourself and your identity. There are as many personalities as there are people, and given that immense diversity, it's natural that we deal with our own position within this world in different ways. From the outside it looks like some people have a much easier time knowing who they are, defining their position in relation to others and their surroundings, and adapting to changes around them. Others seem to struggle much more to define who they are. And while it's true that there are vast differences in how we perceive ourselves, no one is immune to the struggle; some are simply more skilled than others at hiding their struggles. It therefore seems to be a more than adequate purpose in life to find out who you are and be sure of that identity. Since situations around us are ever-changing, this is a purpose that by definition will take all of your life.

Christians struggle with that as well, but we don't think this is the purpose of life. Why? Because for us, the self is not at the center of everything. For us, God is at the center, and the self has its true identity only in relation to God.

Again, this doesn't mean that the actual Christians you know have conquered that struggle. Your Christian friends might be lacking a sense of identity as much as you; they may struggle with their relationships with people and in their response to the many causes that surround them.

But independent of the actual ability or disability of many Christians to let go of ourselves as the center of the universe, the fact is that one of the very central tenets of

Christianity is that the center and the very reason for the universe is God.

Think about what that means: In the Christian worldview, the world is neither centered around you nor is it centered around impersonal principles—such as love and peace or dominance and hierarchy—but around God who created the universe as he saw fit and who continues to be actively involved in every single aspect of that universe and its inhabitants. Oddly enough, he has selected one particular group among all of his creation—human beings—as something special, and he continues to communicate with us by various means. More on that elsewhere.

So, to come back to the meaning of life: It's presumptuous for anyone to give in just a couple of sentences an answer to what philosophers, dreamers, and poets have been searching for as long as people have existed, but Christians would likely agree that the first part of an answer would have to do with focus on God. God is at the center of the Christian's universe, and therefore the Christian life

The world is neither centered around you nor is it centered around impersonal principles—such as love and peace or dominance and hierarchy—but around God who created the universe as he saw fit and who continues to be actively involved in every single aspect of that universe and its inhabitants.

strives to please him, to be at his service. I realize how shockingly subservient that must sound for anyone coming from other traditions, but bear with me for a second. In the Christian worldview, people are not in competition with God. We believe that God has created everything, including us. Just as a work of art serves the purpose of our pleasure and we use it accordingly, so God uses us. Well, kind of. Since we are not static pieces of art (and sometimes we don't even feel particularly artful), but instead living entities who think of ourselves as having a free will, we are in a much more dynamic relationship with our creator. Unlike an artwork, we can decide not to display all the marks of our maker. But if we do decide to point to our maker, we are not only displaying all of our strength and beauty, but we have found the place that we were intended for.

To be and act like we were individually and specifically intended to be and act happens to be what we're created for. Again, it's individual and specific. We're all different, and purposefully so. To find that place where we're in harmony with what we're intended to be is what our purpose is. Well, the beginning of our purpose. What that will look like eventually is for each of us to find out.

And in the process of doing that we'll build relationships, we'll stand up for what is right, and we'll eventually find out who we specifically are.

We're all different, and purposefully so. To find that place where we're in harmony with what we're intended to be is what our purpose is. Well, the beginning of our purpose. What that will look like eventually is for each of us to find out.

I am truly seen
for who I am

As an adolescent, I felt so unformed, so undefined. The only way I could define myself was by copying others, especially the kids I looked up to. I copied the way they dressed, how they talked—especially how they talked, by using the same "cool" expressions they used—but also their facial expressions and even the way they laughed. I liked the foods they liked, the people they were friends with, and the musicians they listened to. It wasn't that all this made me happy or even satisfied me; I knew even then that it was simply a survival strategy. I felt like I was drowning in all the different personas I tried on, while deep inside I felt like I was nobody. I didn't see any depth in myself, any place that

I could reach down and find my own personality traits, so I had to adopt those of others.
But I knew they didn't quite "fit"—they felt
too big, too cool, too mature. In reality, they
simply weren't me.

As adults, our lives might not be as obvi-
ously painful and lonely in our search for who
we are, but still I think many of us display
very similar attitudes. We continuously look
at others and evaluate ourselves in relation
to them and their achievements or failures.
We share gossip about others' failures so we
can define ourselves as superior. We study
our over-achieving friends and neighbors to
understand what they did or didn't do. Maybe
most telling of all, we *celebrate* celebrities.
Think about it: What does the current crop
of celebrated actors, social media influencers,
musicians, and royalty of countries we don't
live in have to do with us? Exactly just as
much as the "cool" people did with me.

And then there are of course people we
used to be close to, whom we admired for
who they were—or, probably better, who

we thought they were. And when it became apparent that they are just as fallible as us, the injury that we felt went so much deeper than that one lost relationship. It seemed like our faith in humanity as a whole was shaken.

Very few of us don't look to others for guidance. That's not surprising. Our nature is to be social, and part of being social is aligning ourselves with others and adapting our patterns of behavior to function in society. We notice this most when we travel or move to a different country. The term "culture shock" is really just the lag in our adaptation to a new social environment. So adaptation is a positive thing; it's a necessary part of living in harmony with our environment.

Very few of us don't look to others for guidance. That's not surprising. Our nature is to be social, and part of being social is aligning ourselves with others and adapting our patterns of behavior to function in society.

Adaptation becomes a problem, however, when it morphs into a quasi-worship of certain groups of people or individuals. The tabloids along the lanes to your supermarket register or the Instagram accounts with millions of followers speak clearly and outrageously about who many of us are attempting to live up to. As I write this, Instagram's highest-paid star was able to charge more than $1 million per Instagram post by selling lifestyle products to his almost 200 million followers. We all know I could keep throwing out similar numbers and statistics proving the power celebrities wield over our lives.

Of course, celebrities can range from actors, pop stars, and reality TV stars to more cerebral academics, writers, philosophers, and spiritual guides. We can learn from all of them, but the problem is that each and every one will disappoint us at some point. How can we know that? Because we're experts. Experts in failure. We have our own lives to look at. Granted, the more the personality of the celebrity is curated for public consumption, the longer it will take for disappointment to set in. But we know that we will be disappointed at some point because there is no one person who will always be successful in fulfilling all expectations.

And what relevance does it have for us, even during the brief period of time when that person still fulfills our expectations? Does this hero worship help us even then? Perhaps only in showing us that at least someone has it all together, is happy and successful—and that we can vicariously join in that success by purchasing their products, buying their books, and watching their movies. Aside from that, we're left behind.

Here's what's different for Christians. The Bible is a book about people and their relationships with God. If you count everyone who is mentioned in the Bible by name, there are more than 4,000 people. While many of them are never talked about in great detail, they all share this characteristic: at their core, they're ultimately failures. The Bible is oddly and brutally honest about people trying to build their relationships with God (or desperately trying not to have a relationship with God) and alternately succeeding and failing. Depending on your viewpoint, it's either aggravating to read this or extremely comforting. Not even in the Bible can we find many people with stellar success stories.

But there is one exception.

The second part of the Bible, the New Testament, introduces Jesus, God in human form, and remarkably, he is described as someone who did not mess up. The four accounts of Jesus' life each comprise between 40 and 70 pages on a regular printed page. They don't describe the life of someone who had completely adapted to society or whose life was free of conflict. In fact, it's just the opposite. So much so, and you know this even if you've never touched a Bible, that he would eventually be killed.

But there are two remarkable things in Jesus's life that Christians try to model their lives on. The first is how he lived, how he challenged the people around him and the society he lived in. Some of his actions, attitudes, and teachings are anything but easy to understand, but by reading about them and studying them over and over we understand that they're driven by one common denominator: love.

The other thing is that Jesus promised his disciples—and in an extended sense us—that these eyewitness accounts would not be the only roadmap to guide us. Instead he promised us a "helper" (he called it the Holy Spirit) to guide us as we emulate him. This especially is what sets Christians apart from everyone else. Christians believe—and when I say "believe" I don't mean believe in the sense of "I believe it could rain tomorrow," but a kind of belief that equals or surpasses "knowing"—that we have been given a helper who supports us in our lifelong quest to become like Jesus. This helper assists us to get up when we stumble, encourages us when we try, and celebrates with us when we succeed.

If you've never encountered this concept it

Christians believe that we have been given a helper who supports us in our lifelong quest to become like Jesus. This helper assists us to get up when we stumble, encourages us when we try, and celebrates with us when we succeed.

may sound outlandish, maybe even like wishful thinking, but it's hard to imagine not seeing the advantage of having someone to emulate who never failed, whose actions were driven by love, and who has given his followers a supernatural gift that communicates with them in the most intimate manner about the most important details of their lives.

This begs the question: Why are Christians not more remarkable, if they really have this superior role model and a supernatural spirit who guides their lives?

That's a question that should make every Christian cringe. The short answer is because we're holding back. We know that we are supernaturally inhabited by Jesus's spirit, and yet we spend an extraordinary amount of time pushing back against him. We have too much pride to say: "This thing I just accomplished is not mine but God's." We might actually say those words because it's "the right thing to say." But do we really believe it? Many don't.

Or let me explain it like this: We've all probably encountered the strong will of a two- or three-year-old when they *really* wanted to do a certain task. Every onlooker knows it's not going to be accomplished particularly successfully (best-case scenario: it's cute and provides a nice learning experience; worst case: the result will be disastrous and also provide a learning experience). Still, the parents might give them free rein, either because they're embarrassed or exhausted or maybe they really believe in the value of that learning experience.

It's kind of like that with the Christian and the Holy Spirit. It's entirely possible that God could do all kinds of remarkable things through us, but he really is less interested in those remarkable things and more concerned with us and our development—just like the parents with their toddler. One unfortunate difference is that the child will likely mature and largely grow out of it, and some Christians never do. Those who do experience growth encounter a beautiful kind of freedom, though: the freedom of not having to claim responsibility for their achievements since they understand that the best thing they did was not stand in the way of God working through them. The vast majority of Christians fall somewhere in the middle, where they sometimes have the mind of a three-year-old and sometimes are past that age. The problem is that others, especially those who are not Christians, tend to notice the failed attempts and the mess they create more than the frictionless successful ones.

And here is one other thing that I—and maybe you—can take away from all of this. If God is not interested in the remarkable things we can do and is instead invested in us becoming, well, us, then any kind of hierarchy related to the value of people cannot exist for God. In turn, for me as a Christian who strives to be like God in human form, this means that I have to (and want to!) believe in a radical kind of equality.

You might have frowned when I claimed earlier, "One of the hallmarks of the Christian faith is equality between genders, poor and rich, people from different origins and different levels of education." Perhaps you thought of some specific churches that don't seem to

If God is not interested in the remarkable things we can do and is instead invested in us becoming, well, us, then any kind of hierarchy related to the value of people cannot exist for God. In turn, for me as a Christian who strives to be like God in human form, this means that I have to (and want to!) believe in a radical kind of equality.

embrace gender-equality. Or examples you've witnessed of unequal treatment of the poor or downtrodden by some Christians or even churches. That and much more may well be true, but I know this: It is an unshakable foundation of the Christian faith that the person living in a broken-down car is held in the same regard by God—and should be by any Christian—as the wealthy in their splendid homes; the counter-cultural rebel is loved as much as the smooth cultural icon; the white male as much as the black or brown female; and the broken as much as the healthy and strong.

At this point it's probably become clear that I have personally failed a thousand times in this. I have condemned people in my mind and I have looked down on them. I have looked up to others and regarded them as implicitly better than me (or you). But in almost as many times as I have failed, I have been able to eventually shake off this illusion of hierarchy and look at others through the radical (and real!) sense of equality that I as a

Christian am privileged to have. And, though not nearly often enough, I was then able to treat them that way as well.

Being a Christian means knowing that I am loved infinitely. You are, too. Everyone is. And since that's all that counts, that makes us all completely equal in our value.

I understand and live fully in my place in the world

What do humans represent in this world? Some, especially at this point in history, would answer that question by saying that humans are the single most destructive force. Others would say we are the most intelligent, creative, and dominant species on earth. If you think about it, these answers are very similar. Both focus on our supreme sophistication; it's just that one sees it as a force for evil, and the other as a good or at least neutral force.

But step back from this concept of human sophistication and take a look at yourself. . . .

Are you done?

Your self-examination likely looks as bleak to you as mine does to me. We're really not all that sophisticated. Sure, we have some intelligence and creativity, but it's wrapped in a less than attractive package. I have conflicting and often despicable thoughts and emotions, which guide my actions and desires, which are sometimes good (as far as my aspirations go) but are often the exact opposite of that, and at best more or less neutral. Now, I readily admit that others might operate at a much higher level with a much better outcome. But my strong feeling is that the majority of people fall into my category.

So then, is this the best life has to offer? As I'm writing this, I'm looking into a sunny October morning which lights up the infinite number of colors between the palest of green and darkest of browns in front of my windows. It's unspeakably beautiful and glorious.

And we are the best there is?

It seems to me that ethically, creatively, and productively, our sophistication lies in our ability to acknowledge the intricacy of the world around us and then understand that we fall short of that. In other words, both emotionally and logically it seems very, very unlikely that there is no entity more sophisticated and capable than we are—whether that being exists on our own or an entirely different plane.

It rubs wrongly against my sense of humility and reality that I—or individually or collectively any of my fellow human beings—should or could be the undisputed pinnacle of everything that exists. Clearly, humans are very capable—for good and for bad. We excel in understanding just enough about our environments to utilize them in a way that is immediately in our favor.

But we neither understand everything around us completely—certainly as far as the consequences of how we relate to our environment—nor are we able to re-create anything that comes close to it. Despite our apparent supremacy, we are clearly and significantly limited. This is true for technical capabilities as well as for judgment and ethical prowess. We understand that there are ethics—and this differentiates us from anything else on this planet—but we constantly fall short of living by those standards, both individually and as a community.

We clearly recognize greatness on a variety of levels. We know that the natural world is intricately sophisticated. We know how to utilize increasingly more components of the world around us. We recognize and celebrate beauty around us. We understand and argue that ethical living is desirable. But we are not capable of either fully adhering to those standards or re-creating any of the beauty around us.

It's like there are kernels of all of this within us. And while these are powerful, they're

Despite our apparent supremacy, we are clearly and significantly limited. We understand that there are ethics—and this differentiates us from anything else on this planet—but we constantly fall short of living by those standards, both individually and as a community.

unformed. They exist only in the very infant stages of what they could be. No matter how hard we try, we won't be able to fully form them or witness them being formed within us.

Here is what Christians believe: In virtually any present or historical society, God comes into play if and when that society realizes that if there is unformed there must also be formed, if there is imperfect there must also be perfect, if there is attempt there must also be achievement.

Again, Christians say that we are made in the image of God. As I mentioned earlier, this doesn't mean that we are made to look like God or exist on the same plane as God. But it means that those kernels in us—the ones we recognize but can't perfect—are fully grown, matured, and perfected in God. Christians believe that these kernels within us are an opportunity to look for the perfected coun- terpart—especially once we individually and collectively realize that it can't be formed or achieved within us.

I can celebrate
and protect
beauty
even though
I believe the
world has an
expiration date

Like non-Christians, Christians are confronted with difficult concepts, even seeming paradoxes. Here is one of the most glaring: Christians believe that there is an expiration date to this earth. We believe that there will one day be a world where fully loving people will live with God in complete harmony.

We have differing opinions on where that place might be (or even if it is a "place" as you and I define "place"), but we do agree that there are going to be times of upheaval and destruction on this earth. You don't have to be a prophet to see this already happening all around us. (This isn't to say that the "end times are near." Despite what you might hear from some radio or TV personalities, most Christians hold firm in the belief that we don't know when those events are going to take place.)

It might seem easy to conclude that while I would not proactively want to take part in the destruction around me, there also really doesn't seem to be much of a reason to stop others from being destructive. It's just the course of the inevitable anyway.

And yet, that's not how many Christians view the world and themselves in it.

So, yes, it's a paradox, not unlike the human experience that knows there is death at the end of life but still tries to prolong it in the most comfortable way with the means provided by medicine and loved ones.

Christians believe that this earth, our habitat, is ours to take care of. Aside from forces that are not within human control—such as large natural or cosmic events (like earthquakes or a collision with an astronomical object)—Christians believe that we are put into place to maintain the earth, to become caretakers of the earth.

"Well, wait!" you (and many others) might say. "Really? Many of the Christian churches I know are not particularly known for their environmental causes. And neither are the people who attend there."

And you'd be right. Overall, the church hasn't shown its greatest strength when it comes to this topic, certainly not here in the US.

I think there are two reasons for that.

The first is that it's simply a failure of many local churches and Christians to give this part of their Christian commitment the proper weight. And this is likely connected with another failure—the politicization of many churches, with the environment kidnapped as a political issue rather than what it really is: taking care of our home. Especially (and ironically), urban churches and Christians tend to place greater value on preserving the world they live in, but there are fewer than there should be. And that's the failure part.

There is another reason behind why churches are typically not in the forefront of causes like protecting the environment.

Churches are not interest-based (as we already discussed). Christians understand churches to be a representation or reflection of Jesus on earth. And while this might sound a little obscure, the point is that churches are supposed to represent the whole of God and not a part. Taking care of the earth is a very important and unfortunately much-overlooked component of that charge, but it still can't be the only cause the church pursues.

But this book is not so much about the church and its failures as it is about why there is an "advantage" to being a Christian, including how we relate to the natural world around us.

If you don't mind, I'd like to take you on a little personal journey to explain why my Christian faith prompts in me a strong urge to uphold the natural world. It might seem like a roundabout way of getting to where others might arrive by a sense of responsibility ("We need to protect the earth to give our children a place to live"), but I think it's just as meaningful and maybe even more pertinent for a person of faith. For me it has to do with beauty.

I love beauty.

There is rarely a day during which I have not spent a part of my afternoon at my local beach here on the Oregon coast to marvel at its beauty. That in itself is not too surprising: Once something is beautiful in our minds, there's no reason it would ever lose its beauty or we would lose our wonder. But what's remarkable about my infatuation with "my" beach's beauty is that it is never the same as it was the day before or the one before that. There are so many elements that influence the way it presents itself—the tide, the swell and the different levels of the surf, the roaring of the waves and the cries of the seagulls and chirping of the sandpipers, the color of the water, the smell and taste of the salty air, the organic debris scattered on the sand, the new carvings in the sand that the last high tide and the birds' claws have left behind, the many and ever-changing colors of the sky, the intensity of the sun, the cloud formations, and of course the wind and the rain here at the Oregon coast.

These are just some of the many elements that make up what I anticipate every day as I step over the foredune. But here is what's odd: There is no day when I come back to my office afterward and complain about the beach's lack of beauty. There might be days when I wasn't dressed right for the elements, but it's breathtakingly beautiful out there no matter how the range of possibilities is configured.

Sand? Water? Wind? Clouds? Taken each on their own they can be annoying at best and life-threatening at worst—and yet together they form great beauty. A kind of beauty, I would contend, that is not "in the eye of the beholder" but is objectively appreciable by every person (who is not plagued with phobias or illnesses that would stand in the way of appreciation).

By the way, I don't go to the beach by myself. Each day my yellow lab and my dingo come with me. And they love it, too, but for very different reasons, like chasing birds, swimming far out to make contact with the ever-elusive but always beckoning seals, and chowing down on semi-rotten crab legs. But beauty? Not a clue. A large open landfill would be equally (or probably even more) enjoyable to them as the beach.

What is it then that sets our species apart and makes us—generally—agree on some kinds of beauty and not others?

In my Christian eyes, it is because we are specially made to appreciate that kind of beauty. And while natural beauty can be found at so many places, it is always in and of itself perfect and therefore always the *most* beautiful thing.

When I praise the beauty of the place where I live, I like to tell others that "ours" is the most beautiful beach in the world. I know

While natural beauty can be found at so many places, it is always in and of itself perfect and therefore always the most beautiful thing.

that's both true and not true at the same time. There are thousands of other natural places that are more or less preserved from human modification—other beaches, mountains, deserts, forests, lakes, and rivers. There are natural phenomena like sunrise and sunset, rainbows and northern lights, a rose bush, an individual flower, a single petal, or its molecular structure. Someone might have a preference for mountains over the sea or roses over tulips, but we will still agree that our less preferred revelation of beauty is still beautiful.

Interestingly—and tellingly—we can receive beauty but not generate it in an equally unanimously appreciated manner. Consider art. While art and beauty are not synonymous, the creation of beauty has long been one of the drivers of art. And there are certain works of art that many of us will agree on as being beautiful. A poem by Rilke, a fugue by Bach, Michelangelo's paintings in the Sistine Chapel, or the Taj Mahal will be deemed beautiful by many, maybe even the majority of people. But by all? Not even close. And when it then comes to more abstract art, more current music, more experimental literature, and more modern architecture, there is going to be a lot less agreement on their beauty or even their intrinsic value.

Why? Because our sense of beauty only truly and immediately resonates with what God has created. Any human effort ends up needing a translation from its creator's expression of beauty to its recipient's sense of beauty. And "translation" might be an appropriate term here: Someone who is not well-versed in the language of 12-tone music might not enjoy a performance of music by Schönberg. To appreciate manga comics, you need a different skill set than for reading poetry by T.S. Eliot or watching a dance performance by the Martha Graham Dance Company.

Here beauty really is in the eye of the beholder, in a resonance of a sense of beauty (or art) between creator and recipient. When God speaks through his created beauty, we all understand because God simultaneously speaks all of our languages.

Why are we given this overflowing sense that seems so counter to our other more utilitarian senses? Most of our basic senses serve our protection and safety. People afflicted with leprosy are mutilated not by leprosy itself but by the loss of sense and the loss of protection it provides. In the same way, if we can't smell, see, hear, or taste, we are either helpless in those areas or need to compensate by other means.

Our innate sense of beauty is both a sustaining force and a force that wants to be sustained because it fills one of our innermost desires. And that really is my strongest motivation to preserve beauty around me. Yes, there is also environmental justice, which is a driver for many other activist Christians. I share that sense, but I can't say it compels me as much as the need to preserve this gift that has been given to us along with the accompanying understanding of its beauty.

Does this mean that I worship nature? Well, I shudder in awe at the many things I see nature do—how it's expressed in us and

Our innate sense of beauty is both a sustaining force and a force that wants to be sustained because it fills one of our innermost desires. And that really is my strongest motivation to preserve beauty around me.

around us—and I know there's so much we don't even know about. But awe is not the same as worship. I, and other Christians, worship the one who is responsible both for nature and the sense of awe: God.

So how does this work, believing that this world as we know it will cease to exist? It's kind of like parents doing their utmost to teach their children and love them without reservation, even while knowing they might have very little influence on what will become of them in their adult lives. Still, we don't spare any effort to form and shape them according to our sense of responsibility for them when they're still with us. Even if we knew they'd later decide to live their life in a way we might disapprove of, we'd still give it our all, happily. That's how we're hard-wired, just like that sense of beauty and the desire to maintain and protect it.

This is true whether you're a Christian or not. The only difference is that Christians believe there is an expiration date of sorts, one that we're eagerly waiting for because then we'll be in God's presence. At the same time, we are made to take in this present beauty that is beyond ourselves, to celebrate it and make it last, and to have a deep and urgent sense of thankfulness for it.

I find my story
in a larger story

One of the reasons I mentioned why people who are not Christians might dismiss Christianity is that they can't accept that the Bible, a book written 2,000-plus years ago for a completely different people, can have a real impact on someone who lives in the 21st century.

I get the logic of that argument, especially the part about the Bible having been written for a completely different culture. Here's why I think this is not a valid excuse.

The Bible is one long ongoing story that is centered around the relationship of human beings with God. The Bible—about one-third longer than the ultra-long *War and Peace*—is made up of many different parts (called "books"). It is attributed to about 40 authors—some anonymous, some known—and separated into two major parts, the Old and the New Testaments. It was written over a very long period of time—about 1,400 years—in various languages.

Given all that, how could the Bible possibly be a single story?

Christians believe that the Bible is an ongoing story of God's interaction with humanity from the very beginning of humankind to the end of humankind as we know it at some point in the future.

The Bible tells the story of the ups and downs of human attempts to live in some kind of union with God (by following an immense set of rules) or to live independently and apart from God—with the common end result that all of these attempts had less than desirable outcomes.

After myriad failed-attempt stories with their aftermaths and repercussions, a new page is turned in the account of God and humans with the story of Jesus' life, death, and coming back to life. That's the part of the story where all people are offered to return as full and worthy members into God's family by simply accepting the reality of Jesus' life, death, and resurrection.

That's it.

Now this is not all told by one person who has a particular writing style or dramatic flair. Instead, this gargantuan story is told in many ways—from songs to narrations to visions to poems—and often from different viewpoints. What makes this so interesting is that it offers so many "points of entry."

Much of my professional life these days is spent researching and documenting how different cultures see the different parts of the Bible. The part they relate to most easily is often determined by a similar work or set of stories in their own language. It's so fascinating to see that there is virtually no part of the Bible that's not especially liked by at least one group. These sometimes unlikely parts become their entry points into the overall story of God and humanity.

That's why the Bible is best read not straight through from its first page to its last. It's also why the Bible is typically not translated in the order you find in the printed Bible in the bookstore. This great story allows anyone to enter at any point, or more specifically, the point that is right for that person or culture. That's the point where they can start to become engaged and then continue or even re-enter at yet another point.

I'm not writing this to convince you to pick up the Bible and read it. This is a book about the benefits of being a Christian as I see them. But having access to the Bible is one of my most cherished ones.

I realize that the term "story" has been a little too en vogue for the last 20 years or so, but pretend with me that we're starting with a blank slate.

Who are you? Who am I? To a great degree we are made up of stories or events of the past, of narratives that have been passed down to us. These stories about our past are not always made up of words—they can be emotions, opinions, or even murky scenes that we can't see very clearly. What unites them, though, is how they work together to make us who we are. Not only at night when fragments of those stories populate our dreams; by day they also guide our actions. It's not surprising that most therapy consists of dealing with our stories, understanding them, redirecting them, and maybe releasing them.

Just imagine what it means to Christians who believe that the Bible is the authoritative

To a great degree we are made up of stories or events of the past, of narratives that have been passed down to us. These stories about our past are not always made up of words—they can be emotions, opinions, or even murky scenes that we can't see very clearly. What unites them, though, is how they work together to make us who we are.

story of God and humanity. A story that involves thousands of people, covers hundreds of years of history, and spans a number of cultural spheres. Even more importantly, it's a story that involves you. Now, every good story involves the listener or reader. That's what makes it good. But Christians believe that this is the ultimate story, about the one who created humanity—God—and his creation—us. So it naturally goes much deeper than stories like *Anna Karenina* or *The Lord of the Rings*. In fact, once you allow yourself to completely enter into it, to become a part of it, it is *your* story. Why? Because it describes your shortcomings and triumphs in your own attempts to be a friend of God. And then eventually, it offers you a way out. It promises that you don't have to be "good"; you just have to have faith and practice the path of love.

For a few years now I've been on a quest to convince the *Museum of the Bible* in Washington, DC to offer a hands-on exhibit of used and worked-through Bibles. Bibles found in thrift stores. Bibles with broken spines and torn covers. Bibles with hardly a page that is not marked up or commented upon in the margins. Bibles with question marks next to strange and difficult passages and lots of coffee or tea marks bearing witness to the many hours in the early morning or late evening when the reader annotated their own story via the story of the Bible. Bibles that give testimony to the wrestling and loving relationship Christians have with their story. There are not many other books that have been worked over with that kind of intensity. And they offer a powerful witness to the Christian journey with faith.

Christians are (ideally) in an ongoing conversation with God. This can take the form of acknowledging in our minds that God is present anywhere and everywhere and therefore also in the very situation we're in right now. It can be thanking God for joyful moments by muttering it under our breath or in our mind. It can be turning to God in prayer in times of need, sorrow, or just a desire to share. Christians see God answer in a multitude of ways—through other people, events that happen this way or that, the clarity and understanding that was not there before they prayed, or—like you were expecting me to say—by reading the Bible.

Again: In the Christian understanding, the Bible is the story of God and humanity passed down by a variety of authors who were inspired by God. This means that every time I open the Bible I expect to encounter God. In fact, I should be surprised when I don't encounter him. Especially as Christians become more familiar with the Bible, we will more often than not know where in the Bible to turn. Not that we necessarily know *exactly* what we'll find there on the very day we read it, but we know what kind of writing to find where, what part of the story of God and his people to find where, where we can find comfort, where we can have the joy we're experiencing reflected, or where to reassure ourselves of our faith. From this, you might get an idea of how precious and deeply, deeply personal the Bible is for Christians in a way that no other work of any kind could possibly be.

The whole Bible as one long story also has a tremendous impact on how Christians read it. Everything is connected in the story, everything is intertwined—and that is exactly how we read the Bible. There is nothing that stands by itself; everything is somehow related to the whole, often in many ways. It might sound like a lot of work to find those connections, but a) there are many libraries' worth of books written about it, and b) maybe more importantly, there is much joy in seeing this grand story unmask itself step-by-step and day-by-day in the ever-maturing life of the Christian Bible reader.

The Bible is the story of God and humanity passed down by a variety of authors who were inspired by God. This means that every time I open the Bible I expect to encounter God. In fact, I should be surprised when I don't encounter him.

Not only is there a tracing of all the many strands of the story to each other, but there are two strands that every part of the story is guaranteed to have: one that points to Jesus (remember: this is the story of God and humanity resolved through the person of Jesus) and one that points to the reader, to me. I've mentioned that as Christians we become a part of the story of the Bible, and it becomes our story, along with billions of other Christians, past, present, and future. Part of that involvement means that every bit of reading somehow relates to me as the reader. It will have an impact on my understanding of God and therefore myself as I'm reading this.

Confusing?

It sure looks like it when you just read about it without ever having experienced it. But here's a little proof. Virtually everyone reading this book will have people around them who are Christians, many for years or decades or their whole lives. Most of them regularly read their Bibles. There are books and chapters in the Bible that they may have

As Christians we become a part of the story of the Bible, and it becomes our story, along with billions of other Christians, past, present, and future.

read dozens of times (think about the dog-eared Bible exhibition I'm championing). Do you really think they would do that if they didn't benefit from it? Are they displaying other signs of mental impairment in the rest of their lives (aside from the regular amount we all exhibit)? No, they return to the Bible because they benefit from it, because they are continuously fascinated by how this story interconnects to itself, to Jesus, and to their own lives.

Let me add one more thing about the Bible's function for Christians and why it's such a powerful tool if wielded correctly.

Think of the Bible as the gauge Christians use to evaluate every encounter in life. Not by a single and isolated verse or story but as a whole. The Bible is the most tangible of the ways God uses to communicate with humans. In it Christians find out who God is in relation to them and how they can relate with him.

Theoretically that could have been done with a short set of guidelines as well, something like the Ten Commandments or the Beatitudes (those pronouncements of Jesus that start with "Blessed are the poor," etc.). But it's hard to form a close emotional bond with something like that. So while these guidelines are found in the Bible, they are woven into a rich tapestry of stories that correspond to the rich tapestry of facets that make everyone's complex personalities.

If a summary of instructions were all we needed to mature, it seems unlikely that we would need to stay with our parents for two decades or thereabouts before going out on our own. Humans learn slowly. This is partly because life is not a matter of black and white that requires only straightforward answers, and partly because humans are in a constant tension between doing what is (seemingly) good for only me at this moment (the selfishly preferred response) or doing what is good for all people and everything around me (the response that needs a lot of training and reflection to come up with). That's what takes parents a long time to do, and that's why the Bible offers thousands of pages of "training material."

But the Bible is not the only way God communicates with Christians. In fact, there's nothing that can't be used, whether it's the beauty of his creation that can be seen so clearly in the natural world, the genius of the human spirit that we see in art, literature, and music, the presence of God's Spirit that lives in every Christian, or the guidance that the community provides. But all that is exactly why the Bible plays such a big role. All of the other forms of communication are much more intangible. Nature and art can mislead and beckon to be worshipped itself. There are many voices that sound attractive and reasonable. And my community is diverse and often wrong. What then is it all good for? It can all be evaluated by the knowledge and experience that I or those around me have gained from studying the Bible. Christians are assured that every guidance from God will be in accordance with the message of the Bible. And again: Almost everything can be confirmed by isolated Bible passages, and that's why it's important to learn and study the Bible as a whole, allowing that overall wisdom to inform our perception.

It's like this: When we watch a compelling movie, read a stirring book, or listen to uplifting music, we are changed. Certainly during the experience but also afterward—until the experience fades. Reading the Bible is sort of like that, only more powerful, and, if done habitually, more lasting. By regularly encountering God's story with his people, us, we are changed, and that change allows us to communicate with God through so many other venues as well.

And why is it "personal" and "practical"? Because it involves us with all of our minute details. In fact, the question should be, "How could it not be 'personal' and 'practical'?" We've already agreed that faith is so hard to grasp if it's not present in your own life. Yes, you might be able to see some of the workings of faith in other people's lives, but Christians clearly don't have a monopoly on doing the right thing. Once you personally experience faith, you will realize that faith will inhabit every nook and cranny of your mind and identity. This kind of faith is hyper-personal and *has* to be practical because it is concerned with the everyday mundane activities of your life as well as the (seemingly) more important aspects and decisions.

Being a Christian means that everything we do and think can be in communication with God. God, who through his Holy Spirit lives in us, helps and comforts us. Is that truly the case for every single Christian at every single point in their lives? Unfortunately not. Is it always available for every Christian at any point? Yes!

I rediscover meaningful thankfulness

There are plenty of articles and books with titles like "7 Scientifically Proven Benefits of Gratitude That Will Motivate You to Give Thanks Year-Round" (an article in *Forbes Magazine* by Amy Morin). An "attitude of gratitude" is a cliché that many of us have heard so often it feels worn out. But it makes sense. It's great to feel thankful. Who wants to be the person who continues to insist that they deserve everything they have or achieve? Well, let me rephrase that: We all know people who have that attitude, but it's far from being an attractive attitude or state of mind, and most of us prefer to be different than that.

When you think about it more closely, though, thankfulness is much more than an attitude. It really reflects a pattern of behavior or a specific act. You thank *someone*. "Thank" is a transitive verb, which means that it has to have an object (someone to thank). We can thank my neighbor for watching my dog while I'm gone, my teachers for helping shape me into what I have become, and our friends for joining us on the journey. We should do that and should do it much more often.

Needless to say, Christians agree with the need to thank people around us as much as we can (and probably more than we actually do). But there are two differences: Christians *always* have someone to thank, even if another human being was not the source of our gratitude. That someone is God. And if a person was involved, Christians can thank that person *and* feel gratitude that God has made it possible to have that person be part of our lives.

Here's the main distinction for me: When I walk out into a fresh, green spring morning or a warm, multi-colored fall afternoon, I am filled with gladness and thankfulness, and it's a huge difference for me that I am able to direct that thankfulness to the one who created that beauty—God—rather than having those same feelings and offering thanks to no one in particular. There is a difference when I meet a person with whom I know a new friendship is developing and praising my good fortune vs. thanking God who has always known this would come about and arranged for it to happen. Someone who doesn't believe in God sees the fortunate coincidence that no one got hurt badly in the car accident, while I can direct my attention to God after the accident and praise him with a heart that is overflowing with joy.

It's like this: When you thank your friend, parent, or partner for the gift they gave, the wonderful meal they prepared, or their preparations for a harmonious evening, you realize that the giving also gave them joy. The gift, the meal, or the time spent together represent more than their face value. They are tokens of

There is a difference when I meet a person with whom I know a new friendship is developing and praising my good fortune vs. thanking God who has always known this would come about and arranged for it to happen.

love and therefore so much more—to them and to you. Now imagine this in a relationship with someone you can thank for everything, *everything*. This is what it's like to have a God-directed thankfulness for everything in your life.

Everything? I know this is a tall order but, yes, everything. If we believe that God wants the best for us, then as mature Christians we even thank him while things are not going well, because even they will eventually lead to something good. This may seem outrageous, like a cheap cop-out to someone who has not encountered faith, but it provides a good segue to our next amazing advantage. Read on.

I appreciate my life as meaningful

We all share a belief that we are pre-sented with choices in what we do. This is true for small things—like how to respond to a person in a particular situation or what kind of attitude to bring into an encounter—as well as for larger things, like what profession to choose or whom to trust as a true partner and friend.

But even when it comes to these "choices," you and I likely agree that even those are not completely our choice. We might be caught in certain patterns of behavior that feel outside our control. Unless we are very privileged or extremely driven, it is not quite true that we can do anything with our professional lives. And that true-friend or true-partner thing . . .

117

many of us have had our hearts broken or our expectations disappointed at some point.

So there are external circumstances that are outside our control—how we grow up, whether others encourage or disappoint us, if we're able to achieve something we strive for, or simply whether situations go our way or not. You might have a "lucky break" with that new job or friend or a "streak of bad luck" with an accident or a sickness or disease.

The concepts of "good luck" vs. "bad luck" relate either to complete randomness in the world or to a kind of "destiny" that holds the cards in its sleeves, ready to pass them out—or not. Either way, we are subjected to a process or "something" that's out of our control and that has no interest in us. That "thing" might be interested in itself or the process but not in the individual participants of that process—us. So we are left to fend for ourselves. We can organize ourselves (as we do in the form of our family, groups of friends, interest groups, governments, or even large international organizations), but those entities only alleviate (or emphasize) some of the impacts of those lucky or unlucky breaks. Groups of friends can comfort in the case of loss or help us prepare and encourage us for life-changing events (like marriage or childbirth). Interest groups can help change policies, accomplish projects, and help where aid is needed that goes beyond the reach of smaller groups. Families are the core groups we belong to that equip us—or should equip us—with many of our skills, passions, and the most fundamental of support systems (again, ideally).

But no matter how big any organization is, the response to anything that "destiny" throws at us is exactly that: a *response* to an event (like a family member's newly discovered disease or

The concepts of "good luck" vs. "bad luck" relate either to complete randomness in the world or to a kind of "destiny" that holds the cards in its sleeves, ready to pass them out—or not.

the response to a natural disaster) or an attempt to change course before an event happens (like preventing a divorce or mitigating climate change).

While Christians can be part of all these responses, we have access to a way of comprehending or compartmentalizing external events that others likely don't. We don't believe in random chance. Instead, we believe that God is integrally embedded in our lives and in everything we encounter, and is therefore a guiding force behind everything.

If you stop here and think about this statement—that there is no random chance, and everything is guided by God in some way—you might think this sounds ludicrous, on a number of levels. How could it possibly be feasible that God is in everything, especially when I disagree with someone else, or even worse, when bad things happen?

Also, if that were the case, does that mean I really don't have any role to play in what's happening to me? Do I not have any "free will" (a term that I have now already used a number of times and also a favorite term of Christians and theologians)?

This is one of the questions where you and I may come to an impasse. The impasse is composed of an incompatibility in the knowledge, understanding, and realm of experience of beings on completely different planes. One plane is inhabited by people who (in Christian understanding) are created; the other plane belongs to God, the one who created them, the creator. And though this may sound like a weak argument, there's really no other classification for this than a mystery. It has to seem mysterious to us—we whose very nature constantly strives to understand more, we who have already succeeded in understanding so much: There are some things that in their essence we are not made to understand because they are literally beyond us.

In our earlier discussion on gravity, I mentioned that we are dealing with faith and not empirical science. Empirical science has no place for mysteries. It knows only yet-unexplained phenomena. Whenever scientists come to points where they can't explain any further, it is because no one has found a way to make logical sense of those phenomena. Unlike people dealing with questions of faith, however, they are in the enviable position of having a long track record of development in their respective branch of science that will possibly—even likely—find answers. Why? Because the phenomena they are trying to explain are of this world and have no will of their own.

Christian thinkers are in a completely different position. They are trying to make sense of something that is not of this world and is completely self-determined. How, for instance, could God possibly be truly omnipresent (everywhere at the same time)? Or how could he have equipped us with a mind and a reason and a will and yet still seem to be in control?

Clearly, any answer to these contradictory questions, or any framework that would solve those contradictions, has to eventually fail. And Christians have to admit that there are built-in contradictions within our realm of experience that form the basis of these questions. Those are the "mysteries."

This does not mean that Christians don't think, write, and sometimes argue about them, even to a point where churches have split over this. In the midst of the uncertainty and disagreement, is there anything that a large majority of Christians would agree on when it comes to this vexing question of God's interference or guidance?

All Christians believe that *overall* God is in control. Equally, all Christians believe that people have the ability to respond to any circumstance with which we are confronted. There are disagreements about whether that response only seems like a free choice but in reality was determined by God long before. There are also disagreements on why calamities happen, such as natural disasters or painful events like disease and premature death. But there is agreement on the fact that there is evil and death, that each of us is confronted with all kinds of choices, that we will experience hardship, and, again, that overall God is in control.

And this brings us back to how we started this section. For a Christian, life is not a game of chance. Instead, life presents us with choices and challenges, while at the same time God somehow—mysteriously—is in control. And unlike fate, God is not neutral. I don't mean that he prefers one person over the other. No, he is for you and for me and for the person next to us. Whether he presents challenges to us or allows those to happen, anything that does happen bears the possibility for us to learn and to grow.

We'll talk more about those challenges when I write about suffering later, but for now here's what I'd like to convey: The life I live as a Christian is not always easy, but it's designed for me to grow into someone more like the only one I really want to resemble: Jesus.

I already talked about the Bible as the book that contains a story in which Christians will find themselves—possibly anywhere, but

For a Christian, life is not a game of chance. Instead, life presents us with choices and challenges, while at the same time God somehow—mysteriously—is in control. And unlike fate, God is not neutral. I don't mean that he prefers one person over the other. No, he is for you and for me and for the person next to us.

most certainly in the person of Jesus Christ. Another open book, one that is even more personal, is our own individual lives. Christians believe that God communicates personally through everything. This means that the life of a person who believes in God becomes the empty pages that God fills through communication with the person associated with that life.

I realize that there are at least two foreign concepts here for non-Christians. First, the inelegant "person associated with that life."

As clunky as this wording might be, Christians do indeed see a difference between their lives and their selves. Yes, we live those lives, but we also believe that these very short lives are really only a blip within our eternal life. Our current lives are only a preamble. There is a very clear difference between my life and me. Clearly, this doesn't mean that I am not responsible for my actions. I am still challenged to live my life filled with love and compassion for people around me. But there is an overwhelming sense that my physical self is very temporary, and the space I inhabit is like a mist—real, but fleeting.

The other curious part of the description above is those empty pages in a book. Aren't those pages anything but empty? Didn't my family and my environment as I grew up, my friends and the experiences as I continued life fill those pages, sometimes more than I wanted? In fact, it seems awfully difficult to

There is a very clear difference between my life and me.

find enough space in and between the tracks of my ongoing life to add anything new, or anything that would meaningfully alter the script that seems to determine so much of what I do.

Yes, in many ways we are products of what we have experienced and the decisions we or others made in the past. That's true for everyone, Christian or not. But again, Christians are in that strange position of living our lives but not completely owning those lives. Ultimately, our lives are owned by God, who has the ultimate right of authorship on that book of life. And it's a right he continues to claim and use. For Christians, this means that there is great excitement and anticipation in the way our lives unfold. Yes, we are living those lives and making decisions that steer our lives, but within all that God's script talks and communicates and helps make those very decisions.

A palimpsest was an ancient manuscript memorialized on material that was deemed valuable enough to be used for more than one layer of writing. When the material, often animal skin, was to be reused, the existing layer of writing was scraped off to make room for a new layer. Today these palimpsests are an important source for researching ancient texts because new technology is able to make the various erased layers visible again. With an important difference, this is kind of how Christians see their lives: God writes the underlying layer, which communicates with and informs the upper layer produced by the person and its environment; however, just like with the palimpsest, only the upper layer—the actions and responses of the individual—is visible at first glance.

Our lives are owned by God, who has the ultimate right of authorship on that book of life. And it's a right he continues to claim and use.

I experience
true forgiveness

Forgiveness might be the most complex and challenging action we can do for each other, and maybe more importantly, for ourselves.

Not everyone agrees with this particular emphasis on the nature of forgiveness, but I do. I have carried the burden of unforgiven deeds, thoughts, and interactions for years and decades; it has eaten me up—and it still sometimes rears its ugly head.

I mentioned above that I work to build a free online tool called *Translation Insights & Perspectives*, a massive web-based collection of words, concepts, and phrases from the Bible translated into hundreds of languages and

*Forgiveness is something
that frees me, unstrings me,
something that enables me to
turn my back on something in my
past that keeps me in chains.*

back-translated into English. Especially for concepts that are difficult to understand, it's very powerful to see how other languages and cultures process those ideas and how the wisdom of that process can aid us in our own understanding.

It's been really helpful for me to study just a few of the Bible's back-translations for "forgive" or "forgiveness":

- to give back

- to wipe out

- to be released

- to turn your back on

- to unstring someone from your heart

This little list builds a helpful scaffold I can climb to mount an otherwise insurmountable challenge.

It tells me that forgiveness is something that frees me, unstrings me, something that enables me to turn my back on something in my past that keeps me in chains. I find it remarkable that in those last three concepts listed above it's about me rather than the person I might have to forgive or ask for forgiveness. Clearly, one aspect of forgiveness is about going to another person and humbling myself or hoping the person might humble themselves—but that's only the start. It might be difficult and, well, humbling to ask for forgiveness, but it's my experience that there's no automatic mechanism to immediately lift the burden I've been carrying for such a long time. And clearly in a case where I've done something I feel guilty about—in relation to someone else, to myself, or maybe even to someone who will never be accessible—that burden's release will have to be negotiated within myself.

Why do I keep harping on about this? Because Christianity mirrors that concept of inner negotiation. Only the inner negotiation becomes an interaction with God.

Why?

Because at the very moment of recognizing God, the newly made Christian asks for forgiveness—for everything that has separated them from God in the past, and for all the unforgiveness that separates them now.

I can assure you that there's a fundamental difference between coming to terms within yourself and essentially forgiving yourself vs. asking forgiveness of someone who truly has the power to forgive. Forgiving yourself is important—for the shame you feel because of what someone else did to you, for the guilt and anger caused by your inability to forgive someone else, or, maybe the most obvious, for something you did that was contrary to your code of ethics. But asking for that forgiveness from someone you believe truly has the power to forgive you and—most mind-bogglingly— is willing to do it immediately and without any restrictions is a completely new level of freedom. You may still have to do some work yourself—especially when it comes to mending or releasing relationships—but God's forgiveness provides a deep assurance that will eventually carry you through to complete forgiveness.

Eventually?

Well, you'll remember I mentioned my own ongoing struggle to completely accept forgiveness. People who are wired like me will take more time to completely heal. But I can't imagine what I would look like if I weren't assured of God's forgiveness—every time, time and time again.

At the beginning of the book, I promised to talk about the advantages of being a Christian, of having an ongoing relationship with God.

God's forgiveness provides a deep assurance that will eventually carry you through to complete forgiveness.

Counting on God's forgiveness may be the most liberating component in the arsenal of advantages that being a Christian allows me to access.

I begin to understand the role of suffering

The two most prominent accusations I've heard against the Christian faith are these: Christians are hypocrites, and how could a loving God allow suffering. We already addressed the hypocrisy allegation. I agree: Christians are hypocrites, likely even more so than others because we measure ourselves and are measured by others against complete perfection—God. We can only fall short in that comparison. On top of that, we not only fail to jump that unreachable hurdle but many reachable ones as well.

I also completely understand the suffering accusation, but I think I have an answer (at least one that satisfies me). This answer allows me as a Christian to view—and to experience—suffering as something difficult, but at the same time as something that is consistent with the God I believe in and which does not diminish his love for me and for you.

Christians believe that in the metaphysical realm of God there is no suffering. Or, more specifically, there is no death. Death is the ultimate reminder of suffering in the Christian world view. I think almost everyone would agree with that. From the moment we're born, we're moving toward the day we die. Most fortunately, as newborns we're not aware of this, and somehow miraculously our parents aren't either (if they were, there would be a lot fewer children. . .).

Biologically speaking, of course, the process of decay doesn't start until a little later. People reach their athletic peak somewhere in their twenties or early thirties. And while it's true that overachieving "athletic" abilities don't really mean much for the majority of people, it shows that the "aging" of our bodies starts long before it becomes noticeable for most of us.

It's hard to say with any certainty, but we humans are likely alone in this anticipation of the end of our lives, or—as Christians and followers of many other religions would say—our earthly lives. I'm not sure animals are surprised by their weakening bodies as they age, but I doubt they expect it. I also doubt they consider that it will eventually lead to death—until maybe the inevitable is the only possible form of reality. We are different. Although humans are living longer than ever before in many parts of the world, the fear of dying is not diminished. In fact, it actually might be increasing, at least in the form of worry about material, mental, and physical well-being in old age.

But regardless, from the moment we are born, a clock starts ticking. This clock might run for just a few hours or a few years, but it will likely continue for 70 or 80 years. The closer we get to the clock running out, the less enabled we'll become—at least physically, probably in the form of disease. From any perspective, this is an outline of suffering.

And while we as a species have become very good at battling the many life-threatening diseases that occur between the time we were born and the time we die, we always eventually fail.

There is also death brought on suddenly through accident or violence, but it is still suffering, certainly for those who are left behind. This, in fact, may cause a more profound and deep suffering.

Can all suffering in life be traced back to the fact that we eventually die?

To answer that, let's look at why Christians believe humans die. We believe there was at

Although humans are living longer than ever before in many parts of the world, the fear of dying is not diminished. In fact, it actually might be increasing, at least in the form of worry about material, mental, and physical well-being in old age.

one point a state that was devoid of decay—no aging, and certainly no death. In the Christian understanding, this state is what we'll return to after death, where there will be no more death and no more suffering.

According to Christian belief, the reason for the loss of this first state of non-decay is, essentially, a willful break from the union between humans and God. This is what Christians call "sin"—or more precisely, "original sin": a turning away from a union between the maker and his creation (humans and the environment they lived in) by the creation's lack of trust in the creator's good intentions. This event, described in the Bible story of the Garden of Eden (Christians differ on whether this description is metaphorical or literal), set everything else into motion: disease, death, birth (wonderful but also painful), and laborious survival. God offered a return to the state of non-decay to anyone who was able to consistently maintain that original union based on complete trust and obedience to a set of ethical and religious rules, but according to the Bible and also to common sense, no one was able to succeed in the midst of a life filled with suffering and brokenness. Instead, Jesus—God in human form—publicly and demonstrably took on suffering by allowing himself to be tortured to death and then return to life a few days later, promising anyone who would put their trust in him a return into the family of God. This represents a radical turning point: Because the power of death was broken by Jesus' coming back to life, the power of suffering has symbolically—and actually in the life after death that Christians believe in—been broken. This in turn makes forgiveness (love) stronger than failure (sin). So while the old system of displaying trust in God was by not failing to obey rules, now it is open to forgiveness and a slate that is continuously being wiped clean. This in turn makes it possible to live in an eternal union with God.

Phew!

You may have been confused, amused, or simply frustrated when you read this. I feel it's important to tell you all this, though, to show you how much the concept of suffering really is at the center of the Christian faith. It's not the ultimate answer. In fact, it's not an answer at all, but it is a reality. The ultimate expression of suffering is death and the path toward it. Other forms of suffering that are not immediately related to death in the Christian understanding are related to it in the sense that they have the same root cause: a willful and continued turning away from union with God. To put it in a more commonly used term: selfishness, which in turn underlies virtually every kind of conflict. This holds true for the original separation from God, the moment that disease and death was introduced, as well as ongoing acts of selfishness that might victimize others.

The concept of suffering really is at the center of the Christian faith. It's not the ultimate answer. In fact, it's not an answer at all, but it is a reality.

All this being said, the charge that wide-spread suffering negates a loving God is all too real and understandable. And rather than hitting people who are suffering with a barrage of the religious-philosophical framework above, there are two primary responses that Christians have to suffering: love and trust in God.

This may not sound too profound, but in practice it's very powerful. Elsewhere we talked about the church. Not the church that is solely represented by its spiritual leader, the pastor or priest, but the church that is made up of its members. If there are specific responses to suffering, such as those that can be alleviated with material help, they'll generously help. If they don't have specific answers—as no one does—when a family member of someone inside or outside the church suffers, they often say nothing and instead bring food, go shopping, mow the lawn, walk the dog, or simply sit with the person who is in emotional or physical pain. Most Christians believe there is no specific answer to the question "Why me?" (as asked by the ones who are suffering), so they don't try to answer it, responding instead with love and service. (In case your experience in that category is different, please let me just say this again, with a request for forgiveness: Christians are far from perfect!)

The second primary response, "trust in God," might not necessarily be wise to share with a person who is directly in the midst of great suffering. Still, as Christians we believe it's true: While God is not responsible for suffering, he's able to turn the suffering into something good.

Let me explain this with a personal example: I have multiple sclerosis (MS), a degenerative neurological condition with no cure. I've had it for many years, and though I'm still mobile and able to work, there are plenty of

While God is not responsible for suffering, he's able to turn the suffering into something good.

things that make me suffer: periodic loss of vision and taste, numbness in certain parts of my body and aches and pains in others parts (or sometimes and weirdly the same parts), incontinence, irritability, extreme fatigue, brain fog, and much more. I don't list these things to ask for sympathy, but to make you understand how I'm able to see my disease as something that has enriched my life in many other areas. The most important of these is a compassion toward other people who are suffering. I would not want to live my life without this hard-won compassion, and I would not have this without MS. Does this mean I welcome being sick? I don't really know how to answer that, especially since it's a very theoretical question. But I celebrate what it has done to me in a positive sense.

This clearly is a unique story because it specifically relates to me, but it's representative because this is what Christians believe God is doing through and because of suffering. This is how we trust God in relation to suffering.

I don't have to worry about aging

There is also an aspect of the process of aging and decay that carries promise in the Christian world view: For the Christian, the outlook is not predominantly one of decay and frailty but of growth and maturity. Again, when I say "Christian" I have the "ideal Christian" in mind, the "Jesus-like Christian," the one who most Christians try to aspire to with various levels of success.

The reason for that outlook is ironically based in failure. As I've said before, Christians believe that throughout all of history there has been only one person who lived a life devoid of any shortcomings: Jesus. And the "history" in this case includes the future. According to Christian belief, there never has been anyone else who, solely based on their ability, has been able to live a life completely pleasing to God. And there never will be. For Christians who are following Jesus as the ultimate model of how to live life, this means that we will never be completely successful.

I admit that this in itself doesn't sound particularly attractive. But another way of looking at this fills this very same concept with hope.

Christians try to emulate Jesus. While they will never reach the pinnacle of that endeavor, they're always on their way to that pinnacle. The Christian life is one long process of becoming more and more like Jesus. Now, just to make sure there is no misunderstanding, "becoming like Jesus" does not mean we have to copycat every single character trait we imagine Jesus to have or somehow try to recreate scenes from Jesus's life so we can be just like him. Instead, it means being as radical as Jesus in loving God and the people around us. That's it. (And—spoiler alert—it's really hard.)

To come back to that "process" mentioned above. A process implies that there is movement, progress. And that's exactly what Christians experience throughout their lives (provided that they continuously follow Jesus): They experience growth. A growth that does not peak in their twenties or thirties or even in their forties and fifties. It's a growth that continues to the very last moment of life on this earth, to the very last breath a Christian takes. That's why the Christian life is not one of decline, and age is not something to dread. Yes, physical strength will cease and the mind may not be as sharp. But neither of those is related to faith and the continued growth that is the hallmark of the Christian life.

"Becoming like Jesus" does not mean we have to copycat every single character trait we imagine Jesus to have or somehow try to recreate scenes from Jesus's life so we can be just like him. Instead, it means being as radical as Jesus in loving God and the people around us. That's it.

But still, you might point out, how can you possibly continue to pursue that path if it's littered with so many failures—the times you've failed to love the way Jesus did? The answer to this is rooted in God's forgiveness. As I mentioned before, Christians believe that when we ask God wholeheartedly for forgiveness, he will give that forgiveness right there and then. This means that not only do we have to feel no shame for whatever we asked him to forgive us for, but God will actually "forget" it. It's erased. There's no trace of it. There is one condition, though: The way we're told to ask is with all of our heart. This means we're asking for forgiveness for whatever we've done with the complete desire not to do it again. Even if we might know it's going to be hard or even impossible, our heart has to want it not to happen again.

This really is the key to why the progression toward a better life, even if we never quite get there, makes sense and becomes desirable. It's because there is faith in an all-knowing and perfect God who understands how people tick and pushes them in the right direction. Those people (us) naturally respond with thankfulness to the process of forgiveness and its self-cleaning aspects and the sense of a motion toward a better life.

Let me try to explain it in a different way.

Imagine that everyone in the world is part of an orchestra. Among all the musicians who are playing certain pieces by certain composers according to the way a certain conductor wants them to perform, there has only ever been one violinist or clarinet player or cellist who at all times has been completely in tune, who has played all the notes perfectly, whose pitch has never wavered. Not just for one piece or two, but all the time and without fail.

It's out of this world how that musician is in tune with the composer, the conductor, and the spirit of the music. And it really is. It's not possible for others of the "world orchestra" to achieve that perfection, but it *is* possible for them to become better and better, becoming ever more like her. Needless to say this takes practice—in fact, a whole life's worth of practice. If you talk to musicians who play in ensembles or orchestras, they will tell you how wonderful *and* hard it is. It's hard because it takes so much effort and time and many, many experiences of failure. But it's wonderful because there is progress for each of these hard-working musicians, and there are times (as fleeting as they might be) when this state of complete harmony with composer, conductor, and music is actually reached. And that transcendence more than makes up for the sacrifice.

It's not a perfect illustration, but it might help a little.

I do remember how confused and frustrated I was after I had just become a Christian when I first encountered this concept of "becoming ever better" but not being able to actually reach that goal in this life. It felt so anti-climactic in its unobtainability. I remember feeling that I had just made a decision to radically change my life, and while I knew there was a lot to learn and that I had to mature on many levels, it felt like an unfairly long haul to me.

I'm certain I was not the only one in that part of my Christian faith journey who felt like that. After all, it's very much against what Western societies teach (to differing degrees): You can achieve anything if you only set your mind to it! It's the bread and butter of every motivational speaker.

This "achieve-it" mentality typically refers to attaining relatively static goals: a particular possession, a degree, a behavioral or time-management change (diet, workouts, more time spent with family, etc.), or a change in relationship status (marriage, start of a romantic or best-friend relationship, divorce). What's different with the Christian kind of achievement is that it's a maturation *process*. And as you would expect from any process, especially one of maturation or learning, this is not one without setbacks. Constant ones, in fact. So constant that they are only matched—and happily surpassed—by the number of improvements.

Is this exhausting? It sure looks like it when it's spelled out like that. What makes this not only endurable but for the greatest part joyful is the reward of playing in tune with the conductor and, most importantly, the nature of the "conductor"—God. You see, this whole concept of maturation through a long process of failures and successes would not work with a conductor who is impatient and ready and willing to give up. Christians believe in a God who, as the architect of this framework of improvements and failures, must be forgiving. If it were a suddenly attainable goal, like a flash of enlightenment, to become like Jesus, forgiveness would not to have to play a role in the nature of the Christian God. Because Christianity has a realistic understanding of the stubborn, self-focused nature of human beings, we don't believe in sudden and lasting perfection, so God needs to be love. And this is exactly what it says in the Bible.

So, let's come back to why this long process is an advantage. To switch our metaphor, it's like this: Life is one long process of coming home. While Christians will not reach our home in this life, every day brings us closer.

What's different with the Christian kind of achievement is that it's a maturation process. And as you would expect from any process, especially one of maturation or learning, this is not one without setbacks. Constant ones, in fact. So constant that they are only matched—and happily surpassed—by the number of improvements.

Not because every day is a day less until we die, but because it's another day toward maturity. And while our bodies might get weaker— if we make it into old age—our home with God becomes ever clearer, and with every additional day and hour we have a stronger sense of where we belong.

I can come to terms with death

I've already written a bit about death in one of the previous sections—death as the ultimate evidence that suffering is part of our existence. For Christians, there is another entirely different way to look at death. Christians don't believe that death has the last word. Christians believe that this life on earth is a mere blink compared to our lives in union with God.

While no one knows exactly what that looks like—aside from an absence of death and suffering—it forms an important building block of our faith. You may be thinking, well, that's not believable because it is certainly not imaginable. And indeed, it's something that is obtainable only by faith, which for Christians doesn't mean a lesser reality, just not one that is based on empirical evidence.

But what does this mean for Christians who do have the faith to see that reality? It means that death is a mere stage whose finality relates only to this life we have encountered so far. Death is real, but it's also fleeting.

As I've mentioned so many times before, Christians are just people. We're anything but perfect. We might cling to our lives even when we know we don't have to, or we might give in to a fear of dying, which in turn makes us suffer. But generally speaking, Christians are not afraid to die in the hope—the expectancy—of what comes next.

This in turn implies that several billion people worldwide (the estimated one-third

Christians don't believe that death has the last word. Christians believe that this life on earth is a mere blink compared to our lives in union with God.

of the world's population who considers itself Christian) have a fundamentally different outlook on this all-important matter of finality compared to those who don't and who see death as final.

Think about what that means: Think, for instance, about what it means as far as our ability to love and give. This capacity becomes unlimited when we don't have to worry about ever being paid back. Think about its implications for the suffering we experience through diseases, loss of relationships, financial hardships, or general deterioration. They're still there, but we can view them very differently because of their now very, very temporary nature.

Even though we look forward to life after death, Christians don't reject our lives here and now as unimportant. Instead, the Christian view of the life after death is what drives and motivates this current life. A birds-eye view of Jesus' teachings reveals that though he talked about life after death, the vast majority of his teachings were related to the present life, with the gritty realities of how to love and how to forgive. So rather than being in a waiting mode before entering the eternal presence of God, Christians are—or should be—in an active loving mode, modeling as well as we possibly can what that presence looks like right now. And with every single little step toward the love we imagine God to be like, we ourselves become a little more like God on earth, Jesus. As I said, we'll never attain that goal here on earth, but the hardships of life, the loneliness embedded in all of us, and the apparent randomness and meaninglessness of life find answers right here and right now. Life after death is beautiful to imagine, but this life is rich and beautiful and meaningful as well. Even when it hurts.

Even though we look forward to life after death, Christians don't reject our lives here and now as unimportant. Instead, the Christian view of the life after death is what drives and motivates this current life.

Wrapping it up

For several years I've been talking about starting a project in which leaders of Christian groups could offer an introduction into their practices to people without a religious home. It wouldn't be a theoretical course on the foundations and beliefs of that particular strain of Christianity, but an introduction to how their adherents *practice* their faith: how often and in what manner they pray, how often they get together with others to worship or talk, how they focus on God, how they help one another and others, what kind of projects they participate in, and so on. And then the religious "seekers" would *do* exactly that. They might not believe in the God they're praying to, they might not recognize the new traditions and customs as their own, but they will commit to *practicing* them for two months, nevertheless—to see what happens.

In the process, the seekers would have full access to the leaders of those churches (or knowledgeable representatives) for questions and conversation.

The goal of this exercise? To see if these two months of practice change the seekers. Would it convince them to stay away from that particular Christian strand? Or would it cause an internal change that makes them want to explore the underlying beliefs more deeply? We may never know, but my sense is that the practice would be transformative. In lieu of the actual experiment, I wonder whether I could suggest something similar but less orchestrated.

In this book, I've talked about the benefits of being a Christian:

- finding an answer to our deep and undefined loneliness

- discovering a new and diverse community of people

- seeing a new and reliable purpose in life and a new definition of what it means to have an impact on the world

- believing that life around us and in us is meaningful and relevant

- having someone to look up to

- realistically and humbly appreciating who we are as human beings

- newly appreciating beauty and how it impacts our care for the world around us

- discovering our own story within a much larger story that provides meaning and guidance

- rediscovering thankfulness

- comprehending a whole new concept of forgiveness and the impact it can have on our lives

- recognizing a meaning behind suffering and aging

- understanding death

A list like this underscores the significance of these benefits.

I can't think of any one of those benefits to which someone would say, "Yeah, that one doesn't sound so great. Maybe this or that, but those two I'd rather leave behind." I do understand that someone might read the list, sigh, and say, "Well, it sounds nice, but it's clearly not for me because I just can't believe in God, or at least not the kind of personal God Christians believe in." Of course, if believing in God were so easily attainable, many more would believe.

So here's what I would like to suggest. Maybe it's more of a challenge: Why *don't* you try it out? What do you have to lose? Why not pretend that there's a God and start talking to him? And maybe at some point you might actually talk *with* him.

Really, you might say, play a game of

make-believe? Yes, exactly! Play make-believe and see what happens. Give yourself as
much time as you need to try to pray. Try reading the Bible. Try exploring the churches in
your vicinity to understand how they approach
God. And continue to keep in mind—as I've
said so many times—that churches are full of
people in need, people who are anything but
perfect. So get ready to meet people who are
just as needy as you are.

And by the way, the reason for the existence of so many different churches is this: At
some point in history, sometimes more than
a thousand years ago, existing churches split
(and often continued to split) because they dis-
agreed about how to worship God (there were
other reasons, too, but this was the main one).
Often the splits were painful, but the result is
really quite wonderful because it shows the
enormous complexity and diversity among
Christians.

You might already know about some of
those churches, or about the Christians in
those churches, and think you're certainly not

that kind of religious person. But that's the other beautiful thing about the wide variety of churches. Some churches might shock you (positively or negatively), some might give you a sense of awe, some might feel cold and exclusive, and some might feel warm and inviting.

To come back to the "faith challenge": What exactly is this for? To find out whether the God that I've been writing about in this book is real. Unfortunately, I can't say, "Look at the beauty of nature or this glorious flower or this newborn baby and you will see God." Or "Look at the suffering in the world or the suffering you're experiencing personally and you will recognize God in it." Or "Read this and that section of the Bible and you will finally understand that God is real." God cannot be proven. But God can be experienced. God can be encountered through experience. It can be a long process, but my sense is that you will know when to throw in the towel after you've given it a conscientious try, or when you realize that your pretense is getting less and less pretentious and more about the living and loving God.

Let me knows how it goes. I'm praying for you!

CPSIA information can be obtained
at www.ICGtesting.com
Printed in the USA
LVHW011333091021
699963LV00001B/5

9 781087 987651